The Good Book
Character is the Thing

William Jenkins

The Good Book
Character is the Thing

William Jenkins

William Jenkins Enterprises   2003

William Jenkins Enterprises
P.O. Box 15134
St. Louis MO 63110
Phone: (314) 652-7933
Fax: (314) 533-1850
e-mail: wisdom@mvp.net
www.jenkinsedex.com

ISBN 0-9744822-0-X

Dedication

This work is dedicated to future generations of American children, our most cherished value. It is for them that I have toiled and wish to benefit most from this effort. I dedicate this book to them in memory of their grandparents and great-grandparents who prepared me to work with them, and modeled for me the kind of citizenship and humanity that are needed now in our country more than ever before. I dedicate it in memory of my first high school coach, Mr. George Holloway, who died a few months before this publication was finished, and to all my teachers who helped mold me into a proper human being.

This book is also dedicated to those first ministers and church workers who laid the foundation for my spiritual development, Rev. E. L. Johnson and Rev. E. P. Powell, who died months apart in 2002 after laboring together in the same Christian community for over sixty years, and the dear church ladies who taught me to do my first stage appearance in an Easter program at the tender age of five.

I dedicate this work to the entire World War II generation who paved the way for our present greatness and set this nation on a path to glory unequaled in the annals of human history. And finally, I dedicate it to the ordinary people I have known along this journey who had nothing to give this world but their goodness and decency, and in giving that, gave more to me and to the world than they could have ever imagined.

Acknowledgements

For this book I am indebted to the students I taught during my years in the classroom who made my life as an educator rich and rewarding beyond measure. They not only shared my values, but also helped me gain a greater appreciation for those values and a greater commitment to them. I am indebted to the many veteran educators whom I have met in the schools across the country. Their help has been invaluable as they have made my work their work also. These persons include Lois Johnson, a brilliant and compassionate educator in Montgomery, Alabama, and Jim Wright, a towering figure in education in Columbia, South Carolina. They have extended to me inestimable assistance and advice in the years I have known them, and their accomplishments have been both challenging and inspirational to me.

I am indebted to Lenora Hobbs for her work in the layout of my manuscript, and her careful attention to every detail. I also acknowledge the assistance and encouragement of Ed Harris who believes that my message should be shared with educators across the country, and who has worked to make it happen. I thank Terrell Walker for his endearing friendship and constant pushing for me to do more and reach more people. And a special thanks is accorded to Frank Ward for his tireless promotion of my work at every level of its development. His contribution can not be adequately measured and my gratitude for it can not be adequately expressed. I end this work with a grateful heart, and that gratitude is extended to all who read these words.

Table of Contents

18. Gratitude

19. Humility

20. Loyalty

21. Compassion (Kindness)

22. Worthy Accomplishments

23. Honesty and Integrity in Speech and Deed

24. Courage

25. Virtue

Introduction

"What are you going to be when you grow up?" Has anyone ever asked you that question? If you are a young person and no one has posed that question to you, be prepared because pretty soon people will start asking you, "What are you going to be when you grow up?" As you approach college age, the question will shift to, "What are you going to college to be, or what are you going to major in?" Adults ask these questions of young people because they know that the time to start thinking about what you are going to do as an adult is while you are a child and have time to prepare for it. They also know the truth of a statement I read long ago when I was a child: "You are now becoming what you will one day become." That statement reminded me that whatever I was eventually to become, the process had begun, and the ground work was already being laid, either by design or by default.

The same is true with you. You are in the process of becoming what you will one day become. The seeds of all future fruits of your life are being sown now. You are a work under construction. Older people know the importance of these formative years to future outcomes, so they ask, "What are you going to be when you grow up?"

Too often, however, when people ask you about your future they are talking only about material things, the kind of work you intend to do, the amount of money you want to make, and the general life style you want to have. You, too, may think mainly of those things when you ponder your future. Such things are important, and it is important that you think about them. By doing so you are likely to take your education more seriously and prepare for a better outcome in those areas of your life. Many students waste their time in school only to discover later that they would have had a much better life outcome had they applied themselves more. So it is important to think seriously about the kind of work you will want to do as an adult, and the kind of lifestyle you will want to lead. In other words, what you are going to be when you grow up.

This book, however, is about a bit more than that, or more accurately, it is about that, and more. In addition to preparing to do certain things, you are also in the process of becoming a certain type of person. Therefore, this book poses another important question for your future, "What kind of person are you going to be when you grow up?" What values will you embrace, and how committed will you be to those values? What kind of character are you developing, and what will be the strength and quality of that character? Just as you are building the academic foundation for your future career, you are also building the values foundation for your future character.

In school, there will be a lot of emphasis on what you know, what you are, what you can do, and even on what you have. All of that is good in its place, and school is certainly the place for such things. The sky is the limit for you. There is a road from where you are that leads to just about any of life's destinations, good and bad ones. But wherever you go, you will need the values and character appropriate for that place, or you will not be welcome there, and ultimately will not be allowed to stay, even if you have the knowledge and/or the skills to function at that level. So in addition to the knowledge and skills for high positions, you need the character.

As you increase your knowledge and develop skills, I hope you will give similar attention to your values and character. The people who work with you want you to be good as well as good at something. It has been easier and less controversial for schools to teach you to be good at something than it has been for them to focus on your being good. As a result, in too many instances, young people have been left on their own in becoming good people. But make no mistake about it, there is a premium in our society on character, and for those who want to have good, fulfilling lives, character must not be overlooked.

So I ask you again, "What kind of person do you want to become?" The kind of person you ultimately become will be the result of the values you embrace and the degree to which you commit yourself to those values. As you choose and commit to values, you will develop character. It is hoped that in the pages of this book you will find information that will help you in your exploration of values, and in your understanding of character. This book explores and explains twenty-five of the core values of the American people. These values serve as the foundation of our culture. They are deeply embedded in our institutions, and reflected in the lives of our citizens. The greatness and success of America is as much about values and character as it is about education.

So it is quite important to the future of America that those who become educated have the values and character to match their intellectual development. I wrote this book to encourage you to consider some of the cherished values of the American people, to help you understand character and its relationship to values, and to impress upon you the importance of embracing good values and developing strong character. I hope that the things I have written here will help you become a good, decent, happy, and fulfilled person, as well as a materially successful one.

The Good Book: Character is the Thing

We hear a lot of talk about character in America today. We hear about it in political campaigns, business scandals, and high-profile firings. Much of what is wrong or right with our society is attributed by some to our character. We are even told that we as a nation have character and that the way we act on the world stage is a reflection of our character. As a young person, you are told that you should have character, and that you should be in the process of developing good character. At some point you will be expected to emerge as an adult with this good character that everybody expects of you, but nobody clearly defines what character is and explains to young people how to go about developing it. This book is an effort toward that end. The word "good" in the title refers to character, and the standard for character is the cherished values of the American people. Whoever embraces the values presented in this book and commits to them will be considered to have good character.

Young people who want good character need a standard and guide in pursuing it. You need something on which you can focus your efforts and something by which you can measure your progress. It occurred to me after I started working on this book that apart from what we have traditionally called Christian values, Americans don't have a clear definition for character. We use the word character frequently, but almost never define it. In fact, in all of my years of hearing people use the word character, I can't remember ever hearing anyone define it. We simply assume that to be of good character is to embrace a cluster of values that we have associated with Christianity. So good character in America has meant being a good Christian. I have often heard the expression "good Christian character" as if the two were synonymous. But they are not.

This is not to say that good Christians don't have good character;

many of the persons I know who have demonstrated the very best character were Christians. The point here is that you don't have to be a Christian in order to have character. You don't even have to be a Christian to have good character. People have character whether they are Christian or not. People have character even if they are not religious or do not believe in God. You can have good character or bad character. Technically, character has less to do with whether you are good or bad, than it does with how honestly your behavior reflects your beliefs.

By definition, character is the degree to which a person's actions mirror his/her beliefs or values. It is consistency between what a person is and what he claims to be, and the degree to which he commits himself to his values. Character is faithfully and consistently acting on one's beliefs, whatever those beliefs are. Socrates put it this way: "The shortest and surest way to live with honor in the world, is to be in reality what we would appear to be; all human virtues increase and strengthen themselves by the practice and experience of them."

By definition, and by the wisdom of Socrates you see that character and values are intricately linked. Yet character is a neutral term. Whether your character is good or bad can be measured only through what you believe and how you act on those beliefs. Good character is strong commitment to good values. But character is simply the commitment, and not the values themselves.

So it is important that you understand that your values, whatever they are, will be the content of your character. If the values are bad and you commit to them, then the character will be bad; if the values are good and you live by those good values, you will have good character. Values plus commitment equals character. The better the values and the stronger the commitment, the greater the character. So if you want to be respected in our society as a person of good character, you need to build that character around good values. And according to the statement by Socrates, the more you practice your values the more your life will reflect them and become defined by them. And the more you will become at one with your values.

And exactly what are values? What are adults referring to when they talk to you about your values? What are they trying to pass on to you when they attempt to pass on their values to you? Values, simply put, are those things that we value; they are the things that are important to us. We spend our money and our time on those things, and in time, we give our lives to them.

If we learn to value good things as young people those values almost automatically lead to us becoming good people. To the contrary, if we come to value bad things, it is just as likely that we will become bad people. So values are very important, and choosing good values early is essential to becoming a good person.

If you choose to become a good person, you do not need to look very far to find good values, and good examples of goodness. You see them all around you; in your parents, grandparents, uncles, aunts, teachers, coaches, and many of the people you encounter in your daily life. These are not necessarily famous people, wealthy people, or great people. They are not all educated people or extremely successful people. But they are good and decent Americans because they live by good values and have set examples of goodness for those who know them. In these people you see values that have been passed down from generation to generation and that have served each generation quite well. These values have passed the test of time and have proven to be sufficient for a great people and a great society, and anyone who embraces them will be considered good by the rest of society.

We, in this country, from the very beginning have had a basic set of values that most of our people have embodied and have benefited immensely from having done so. Many of the people who embraced the values were Christians, but the values themselves are not necessarily Christian values. The Jews embraced some of them before Christians adopted them. The Greeks and Romans embraced several of them. Religions and cultures in other parts of the world also embrace some of these values. So they do not belong to the Christian church or any church, or any nation or group. Values belong to anyone who adopts them. And they will work for anyone or any society that puts them to work.

However, nowhere else have these core values been combined and had the results that they have had in the United States. Our values, more than anything else, distinguish us from other countries. They are the foundation for our greatness. Therefore, those of us who care about the country and its future, and care about our young people, want these values to remain a part of American life, and want them to be passed on to each generation of American children. That is certainly true of the twenty-five values that are presented in this book.

These are twenty-five of the most cherished values of the American people. They are the glue that holds our society together. We embraced some of these values from the very beginning; others we grew into, or enlarged upon. We started out valuing freedom and equality, but not for everybody. It took years of protest, agitation, and legislation for blacks and women to have that freedom and equality extended to them. But they now have it. We did not always value our environment to the proper degree, but we came to do so, and now caring for our environment is one of our cherished values.

Our country has always been evolving and moving toward the "more perfect Union" our fore fathers challenged us to become. It has always been becoming what it has now become. This country is a collection of people who have embraced a wonderful set of values, and the strength of the country will always be in proportion to the degree to which the values that made it strong are embraced by its individual citizens. As the values go, so goes the country.

We are a strong nation whose strength is matched by our commitment to justice. We are a rich nation whose wealth is matched by our generosity. We are an ingenious nation whose ingenuity is matched by our sense of responsibility. We are a grand nation whose grandeur is matched by our virtue. We are a daring nation whose daring is matched by our respect for God and what we believe is his purpose for our existence. We are Americans, a good and decent people. We try to reproduce that goodness in every new generation by sharing with them the values that have made us what we are. Anyone who wants to aim for that goodness should consider starting with these values. These following values have served as the hallmarks of American society:

1. Life and human dignity
2. Religion and religious freedom
3. Country and citizenship

4. Personal freedoms
5. Respect for the rights of others
6. Respect for others' property
7. Justice and fair play
8. Motherhood
9. Family
10. Respect for the elderly
11. Taking personal responsibility
12. Diligent and honest work
13. Knowledge
14. Contributing to society (philanthropy)
15. Obeying the rules
16. Respect for authority
17. Taking care of our environment
18. Gratitude
19. Humility
20. Loyalty
21. Compassion (kindness)
22. Worthy accomplishments
23. Honesty and integrity in speech and deed
24. Courage
25. Virtue

These are some of the values or characteristics that are important to Americans. Of course, there are others. Like any list, this list leaves out some items that others would have included, and includes some that others might have omitted. This list is not intended to suggest that these are all of our values, or that all of us value each of these to the same degree. It is just to say that if you could look deep into the souls of Americans, you would find in most of them a considerable appreciation for the values I have listed. I can also assure you that if you have these values and commit yourself to them so that they are reflected in your life, you will probably be well-liked and have great success in life.

In the pages that follow are explanations of each value and a suggestion of how one's character can be built and judged by that value, if he embraces it. As you read through the rest of this book I would like for you to consider each value and determine whether it is valuable to you. If it is valuable to you, I would like for you to think of the Character Component to see whether you are developing your character around this value.

At the end of the discussion of values there is a test that will give you a measure of how important these values are to you and how much your life might be reflecting them. The test is designed to be fun, but there is a serious side to it. It might give you some very important information about how you will be perceived by older people and about what kind of person you are developing into. Now let's explore the values.

Life and Human Dignity

To be what we are, and to become what we are capable of becoming is the only end of life. —*Robert Louis Stevenson*

Our highest value is for life and human dignity. We believe that one should not just live, but live in a state of dignity. We believe that life is a sacred creation and should be honored and respected by all human beings. Human life has dignity, which is the highest degree of importance. Dignity demands that life exist in the highest state of freedom and worth. Human beings can't create life, therefore, we believe that we have no right to destroy it nor do we have the right to demean the dignity of it.

In the last decade there has been a tremendous increase in violence in America, even in our schools. It would appear from these events that our value for human life is not as strong as it once was. It would appear that the young people today do not value human life as much as past generations valued it.

But in spite of the increase in violence in our land, human life is a cherished value in America. We should value, protect, and preserve life. We should also maintain it in its highest state of dignity. Our present dilemma over cloning and stem cell research is just one example of the value we place on human life, and the difficulty of maintaining the dignity of human life amidst the technological advances that we've made and the possibilities that those advances have opened up for us.

We saw a demonstration of our value for human life when the World Trade Center was attacked by terrorists. Firemen, policemen, and ordinary citizens risked their lives, and some gave their lives in heroic efforts to save human life. It was also seen in our universal denouncing of the taking of innocent life to promote any cause, or make any political statement.

People of good character who value human life behave accordingly. They do not put their lives or the lives of others in needless danger. They go out of their way to protect life, and they do whatever they can to prevent the taking of life. Years ago one of my friend's fourteen-year-old son jumped in front of one of his friends and took a bullet that was aimed at the friend. He died in that heroic act. The death of his only son was a terrible blow to my friend. But he told me that he was comforted by the fact that his son had done the noblest thing that a person could do; he had given his life to save a life.

Few of you will be called upon to do such a thing, but you will be presented daily with situations that will give you a chance to show your value for human life and the dignity of human life. Your character will be judged by the way you perform in such cases. If you value human life that value should be seen in the way you live your life. If you believe that human beings have dignity and worth, you should treat every human being with dignity, regardless of the person's place or station in life. The dignity of human beings is attached only to their humanity and not to any of the trappings of the human condition. Therefore, people of good character treat people with dignity even if the people are uneducated, poor, elderly, sickly, different, or powerless. They are dignified human beings and should be treated with respect. If you want good character, and you believe in human dignity, you have to extend that treatment of dignity to every human being. The extent to which you do so will be the extent to which people will see you as having good character.

Rules to Live By

Life and Human Dignity

1. Respect and protect all life.
2. Always wear seat belts.
3. Never endanger or take a human life except in the case of protecting another human life.
4. Maintain life in the most dignified condition.
5. Never drive under the influence of mind-altering substances.
6. Never unnecessarily endanger your life and/or the lives of others.
7. Make every effort to keep friends from driving drunk.
8. Don't bring life into the world irresponsibly.
9. Take good care of the sick and elderly.
10. Maintain good health habits.
11. Don't belittle or make fun of people.
12. Maintain self respect.

Religion and Religious Freedom

Congress shall make no law respecting an establishment of religion or prohibiting the free exercise thereof. —U.S. Constitution, Amendment One

Religious freedom is the freedom "to be or not to be" religious and to be religious in a way that satisfies one's own conscience. Some choose to be religious and others choose not to be. Both are at home in America. It was the quest for religious freedom that brought many of the first Europeans to this land. They came here fleeing religious persecution and state-mandated religion. However, they themselves were a very religious people. But it was to be religion of their own choosing that was to be carried out in a way that was consistent with their conscience rather than a government mandate. Religion and the freedom to practice it as they pleased were so valued by the first Americans that they made it a part of their constitutional rights. They specifically declared that the government shall not interfere with the wholesome practice of religion, nor shall it dictate to any person his choice of religion, or his way of acting out his faith. We Americans may not be as religious as we once were, and may have strayed a bit from the faith of our fathers, but the value we hold for religion and religious freedom is still very strong.

If you value religion and religious freedom your character can be measured by your devotion to your religious beliefs, and by how fairly you extend to others the religious freedom that you demand for yourself. I was brought up in a religious family. My father was a minister. We were expected to go to church and live by the rules of our religion. My parents set good examples for me in that regard. They never missed attending church on Sunday, and they lived by their religious teachings. To this day I am still quite loyal to my religious beliefs and those beliefs impact practically every serious thing that I do.

Even though I am loyal to my religious beliefs, I know that others have a right to have different beliefs or no religious beliefs at all. They respect my beliefs and I respect theirs. Those who insist that others tolerate their religion must be similarly tolerant of the religion of others if they wish to have good character. America is now a land of many religions. In the last two decades we have seen an influx of different religious groups. Our character and commitment to religious freedom will be tested as we are challenged to afford to these new groups the freedoms that we demand for ourselves, assuming that their religion is genuine and their practices are compatible with our culture and security.

Our value for religious freedom does not require that we put ourselves in danger by allowing the proliferation of religious groups that have expressed desires to do us harm. Our tolerance must be tempered by our awareness of others' intolerance for us.

We can strengthen our character by showing tolerance, understanding, and even appreciation for the religious beliefs and practices of others. However, our character is also tested by how loyal we remain to our beliefs as we come in contact with those who have different beliefs.

Rules to Live By

Religion and Religious Freedom

1. Be true to your religious teachings.
2. Support your religious institutions.
3. Properly represent your religious affiliations.
4. Respect others' religions and religious practices.
5. Don't make fun of others' religious customs.
6. Never make fun of other people's religious attire.
7. Don't insist that friends accept your religious beliefs and practices.
8. Remain loyal to your beliefs when confronted by those who have different beliefs.
9. Respect the worship places of other religions.
10. Respect the special observances of other religions.

Country and Citizenship

Ask not what your country can do for you; ask what you can do for your country. —*John F. Kennedy*

The greatest values in the world are worthless if you have no place to practice them. America affords us a place to practice our values. So we value this place, our country. Many Americans believe that ours is the greatest country in the history of the planet. Hundreds risk their lives daily to come here. Those of us who are citizens here are quite fortunate. It is our country and we pledge our allegiance to it. I was taught as a young child to value the country. In my school we started our days with a pledge of allegiance to the flag and country. We also sang patriotic songs that taught us that this country was a gift from God and that we should love it and thank God for  it. The playing of the national anthem before major sporting events and at other large gatherings is a testimonial of the value we hold for our country. The love of country is deeply embedded in American culture.

Character Component

People with good character who love the country protect it when it needs protection from without and from within. They obey the just laws of the country and work to change unjust laws. They become educated so they can participate responsibly in the democratic process. They practice good citizenship and rear their children to be good citizens.They respect and show appreciation to those who defend the country.

As a young adult I used to travel across the country to lecture at colleges and universities. During that time hitchhiking was common. It was much safer back then and people routinely gave rides to hitchhikers. Soldiers regularly hitchhiked home when they were furloughed or discharged from the services. I never passed up a soldier in uniform. I considered giving them rides an honor and an act of patriotism. Since I didn't serve in the armed forces, I considered supporting the soldiers as a way of saying thanks for their service. I have benefited immensely from the contributions of others to this country and I give back in whatever ways I can. I also see teaching as a way to serve the country. Teachers who help develop young people into good citizens are performing a great service to the country. Contributing to the country is an appropriate behavior for a person of good character who loves the country. If you love the country and have good character, your behavior should reflect that love.

Loving the country does not necessarily mean that you show that love exactly as another might. It means that whatever you do must be done out of love for the country. During the Viet Nam War, and more recently during the conflict in Iraq, some people protested for the war out of love for the country while others protested against the war out of what they said was love for the country. Both groups could have had good character if they were acting out of love for the country.

You may show your love for the country simply by getting a good education and preparing yourself to be the best citizen that you can be. Becoming educated is one thing that good patriotic character demands of you at this point.

Rules to Live By

Country and Citizenship

1. Obey the rules.
2. Keep your environment clean.
3. Vote.
4. Get a good education.
5. Pay your taxes.
6. Volunteer.
7. Give to charitable organizations.
8. Prepare to rear responsible children.
9. Respect the flag.
10. Always stand for the national anthem.

Personal Freedoms

But what is freedom? Rightly understood, a universal license to do good. **—Alfred Lord Tennyson**

Our constitution guarantees us certain freedoms and we take those freedoms very seriously. No one has the right to take another's freedom, and no person has a right to use his freedom to infringe upon the freedom of others. Our freedoms are spelled out and guaranteed in the constitution, and even municipalities and states cannot deprive us of any freedoms that are afforded to us by the constitution. In America, freedom is sometimes valued as highly as life itself. In his stirring speech before the framers of the constitution, Patrick Henry said: "I know not what course others may take, but as for me, give me liberty or give me death."

Our love for freedom is evidenced by the price we have paid for it. All of our wars have been waged in the name of freedom —sometimes in other lands to free other people. The American Revolution was fought to free the colonies from the tyranny of Great Britain. The Civil War was fought to free black people from slavery. World Wars I and II, the Korean Conflict, the Viet Nam War, and the war in Iraq were all fought in the name of freedom. More American blood has been shed on the battlefield for freedom than for any other cause. We value freedom. Freedom, more than any other quality, distinguishes America from other countries. Nowhere on earth are people as free as we are and we like it that way.

However, freedom comes with certain responsibilities. Every free person is charged with the responsibility of using his freedom within the context of constitutional intentions. We believe that our freedom has to be exercised with the greatest regard for the freedom of others. Hence, our freedom of speech does not give us the right to spread lies and to speak irresponsibly. Not only does it not permit us to yell fire in a crowded theater, it does not even give us the right to talk loudly enough in the theater to prevent others from hearing the dialogue in the movie.

Since 9/11 some of our personal freedoms may have to be compromised for the safety of the society, but even those compromises are approached with the awareness of the great value we Americans have for our personal freedoms.

Persons of good character who value freedom act responsibly in a free society. They neither abuse their freedoms nor take them for granted, and they stand ready to guard those freedoms when they are threatened.They show their high regard for their freedoms by respecting and honoring those who gained them and those who maintain them.

To value freedom is not simply to value being free, but to value the quality of freedom, and to want it for others as well as for yourself. Therefore, people of character who value freedom don't just promote it for themselves, but for everyone.

The Civil Rights Movement, the Women's Movement, and all of the other movements for greater liberties in America challenged those who believed in freedom to extend to others the freedom that they wanted for themselves. When Martin Luther King, Jr. stated in his "I Have a Dream" speech, "I have a dream that is deeply rooted in the American dream," he was challenging white America to extend to blacks that which they had demanded for themselves.

When women demanded the right to vote and the right to participate equally in the market place and work place they were challenging men to extend to them the rights that they had demanded for themselves. Good character can do no less. If you believe in freedom, your character is revealed by the way you exercise your freedom and the things you do to help others secure theirs.

Rules to Live By

Personal Freedoms

1. Exercise your freedom within intended guide-lines.
2. Be willing to fight for freedom.
3. Be willing to make sacrifices for freedom.
4. Always respect others' rights.
5. Never withhold from others rights that you demand for yourself.
6. Never use your freedom irresponsibly.
7. Be patient with the freedom struggles of others.
8. Don't change rules when your position changes.
9. Respect the rights of others.
10. Respect and support those who secure and maintain your freedom.

Respect for the Rights of Others

We hold these truths to be self evident—that all men are created equal; that they are endowed by their creator with certain inalienable rights; that among these are life, liberty, and the pursuit of happiness. —Thomas Jefferson in the Declaration of Independence

If we are to coexist in harmony in this free society a healthy respect for the rights of others must be maintained. Here that respect has been maintained. We value our rights and we value respecting others' rights.

Respecting others' rights means accepting that they have the right to have those rights and responding accordingly. Our rights are afforded to us by the constitution. We have the right to a trial by a jury of our peers. Those who are arrested have a right to remain silent until a lawyer is present. If they don't have money to hire a lawyer, one is provided for them. These are some of our constitutional rights.

We also have what we refer to as inalienable rights, which are God-given and even the government shouldn't be able to take them away from us. The government respects our God-given rights. Respect for rights is one of our high values. We see our rights directly connected to the rights of others. Therefore, we have to respect and protect others' rights in order to feel secure in our own rights. We further believe that those who do not respect the rights of others do not deserve those rights for themselves.

Young people like to demand and assert their rights. It is a beautiful thing to see people become aware of their rights and exercise those rights with responsibility. As an American citizen you probably have more rights than any other citizen on the planet, and your country goes to a greater extent to protect those rights than does any other country on earth. Good character requires that you use your rights responsibly and extend to others the rights you demand for yourself.

It is poor character when one is willing to withhold from others that which he demands for himself. If you value respecting others' rights, when it comes your time to respect the rights of others, good character demands that you do so. Character often comes down to doing unto others as you would have them do to you. It is living what you say you believe. If you believe it, let it be reflected in your own life. That is good character. Many people selfishly demand rights for themselves that they do not want extended to others. That's bad character.

Rules to Live By

Respect for the Rights of Others

1. Stand up for the rights of others as if they were your own.
2. Never demand rights or privileges for yourself that you would not extend to others.
3. Never disrespect the rights of others.
4. Vote.
5. Don't insist that your friends copy your behavior.
6. Respect "no" from your friends and associates.

Respecting Others' Property

Among the natural rights of the colonists are these: First a right to life, secondly to liberty, thirdly to property. —Samuel Adams

In America personal possessions are precious. Our country thrives because individuals are able to achieve individual goals and acquire personal items and resources. In such a society, those accomplishments  must be respected, honored and protected. Consequently, we place a high value on respecting other's property. To some degree, a person's property is an extension of the person himself/herself. To tamper with one's property without permission is a violation of that person's being. The fact that we have property taxes and several laws protecting property is an indication of the value our society places on property and the respect for one's property. One's maturity is partly judged by one's ability to respect others' property, to leave their things alone.

Today, our respect for others' property has declined. Young people don't have the respect for others' property as Americans did in the past. Today practically everything of value has to be locked and watched. Such was not the case just a couple of decades ago. A car alarm was practically unheard of in my youth. People routinely left their cars unlocked overnight and nobody bothered them. Personal items were left unattended and were not taken. Today is a far cry from those days. The respect for others' property is not as strong. But it is still one of the long held values of the American people.

People who want their own belongings respected and undisturbed by others should show that same respect for the property of others. Not to do so is a sign of bad character. It is bad character to wear your brother or sister's clothes and get upset if they wear anything of yours. Character forming begins very early. Young children who play with their friends' toys but refuse to share their toys are showing bad character. Good character requires that you respect other people's property if you want them to respect yours. Parents and siblings are persons also. You need to respect their property just as you respect other people's property. In fact, most people learn how to respect others' property by being taught in the home to respect the property of parents and siblings.

As in so many other things, character here comes down to doing unto others as you would have them do unto you. If you tamper with your parents' cars and belongings without their permission while insisting that they not bother anything that belongs to you, you are showing bad character. One of the most difficult and most important lessons you can learn is not to bother that which does not belong to you. If you learn that lesson well it may keep you out of a lot of trouble, out of jail, and possibly out of an early grave. And it will be a plus for your character.

There is one other thing about property and character that you should keep in mind. If you take responsibility for somebody else's property you should never turn that responsibility over to another person without the owner's permission. When you borrow something from someone you have no right to let anyone else have any authority over that item without the original owner's permission. To do so is bad character and can get you into some real trouble.

Rules to Live By

Respecting Others' Property

1. Do not take or tamper with anyone else's property with out permission.
2. Don't borrow anything that you can't afford to replace.
3. Respect others' property as you would like for them to respect yours.
4. Never take responsibility for others' property if you are not going to really watch it.
5. Return borrowed items as soon as you finish with them.
6. Never do any more with others' property than they give you permission to do.
7. Never lend borrowed items.
8. Return borrowed items personally and timely.
9. Never be afraid to ask for or give receipts for transactions.
10. Never let your friends drive your parents' cars with out permission.

Justice and Fair Play

We value equal treatment under the law. We are a nation of laws. No one is above the law. Money, power, prestige, fame, nor any other earthly advantage or disadvantage should affect the way the law is applied to a person. We value justice and we want to be treated fairly. We believe that it is right to be treated fairly and that fairness is an entitlement owed to everyone. There is a dual dimension to justice; one dimension is how consequence  is related to deed, and the other dimension is how the consequence is applied to one person as compared to another. For example, not only should a punishment be appropriate for a crime, but should be the same for everyone who commits that crime, all other things being equal. A poor person should not be sentenced to ten years in prison for a crime that a rich person, for commiting the same crime, gets six months' probation. One reason some people give for opposing the death penalty is that some groups are more likely than others to receive it for the same crime. If that is true, then it is unjust.

We believe that the best way to insure justice for ourselves is to have a society wherein everybody receives justice. It was this idea that Martin Luther King expressed when he said, "Injustice anywhere is a threat to justice everywhere." Our laws are just and we attempt to implement them justly.

If a person truly believes in justice his character can be judged by the standards or double standards he has in his relationships with others. When one demands that people be just with him and he is unjust with others, that is bad character. Individuals and nations have character. The character of our nation is judged by how we dispense justice to every one of our citizens. In America the lowliest citizen is to have equal opportunity to be treated justly by the country. And our country is judged by how well it treats even the least among us. So will your character be judged by how just you are with the people with whom you come in contact. Justice is sometimes a tough thing. It requires the very best from us. But if we want good character we must do the just thing even when it hurts us personally.

Rules to Live By

Justice and Fair Play

1. Be an example of justice in your personal behavior.
2. Support justice whenever you have a chance to do so.
3. Use your influence to ensure justice for others.
4. Get the facts before you make judgements.
5. Always use your position or authority justly.
6. Be fair in all your dealings with others.
7. Choose to lose rather than win unfairly.
8. Don't knowingly benefit from injustice.
9. Support justice even when it is unpopular.
10. Return favors.

Motherhood

Mother is the name for God in the lips and hearts of children.
—W. M. Thackery

Americans value parenthood, but we generally attach more sentimentality to motherhood than fatherhood. We see mothers as the channels of creation, the avenues through which life comes into the world. Therefore, women in our society get more respect when they become mothers. The value of motherhood is instilled in children at a very early age. Fathers will sometimes allow their children

 to disrespect them quicker than they will allow them to disrespect their mothers. I grew up in a society that had the highest respect for motherhood. At that time all women were expected to be mothers, so we gave all women that motherly respect. We were not to use foul language in the presence of women. Men did not drink around women, they did not gamble in the presence of women, and they did not even approach women inappropriately in public. To this day I treat women with the utmost respect. However, the young people of today don't seem to have the respect for mothers that was held by older generations. I am appalled and embarrassed by the disrespect that is shown to mothers today. The popularity of rap music and the degrading things that those musicians say about women, coupled with the roles women play in movies and in society, have contributed to the decline of respect for women. But motherhood has been a cherished value in America for a long time and should always be. I would hate to have to live in a society that did not respect women, especially mothers.

Practically everyone wants the women in his or her life to be respected. Good character, however, demands that such respect be extended to other women also. Men of good character respect women even when those women don't seem to respect themselves. I was never allowed to use women's behavior as an excuse for disrespecting them. I was taught that the way I acted toward women was a reflection on my character, not theirs.

However, women who want to be given respect have a responsibility to act in a way that is consistent with the respect they want. I hate to see today's young men disrespect mothers, but I am equally appalled to see some of the things that young ladies do and the language they use. I believe that both contribute to the way young men act toward them.

Since society values mothers, mothers who want that value and respect should carry themselves accordingly. We value mothers because of what they mean to society. We hold them to high standards and look up to them. Ladies who would deserve such high standards need to conduct themselves in ways worthy of that respect.

Men who value motherhood treat their wives with greater respect and dignity once those wives become mothers. Men who value motherhood are respectful to women in general because they want other men to be respectful of their mothers. When I was a child the quickest way to start a fight was to say something bad about another child's mother. Children then had an unyielding loyalty to their mothers. They were not disrespectful to their mothers. Toward the end of my teaching career, it was popular among my students to rebel against their parents, especially their mothers, around the age of sixteen or seventeen. Whenever it was brought to my attention, I discouraged it. One day after one of my remarks against disrespecting mothers, one of my students asked me,

"Didn't you rebel against your mother when you were our age?" I told him no. Years later I wrote the following poem to elaborate upon why.

No, I Did Not Rebel Against My Mama

No, I did not rebel against my mama
For too many times she was up preparing my breakfast while I was still asleep.
She would turn on the radio so I could hear a sermon before I spoke a word.
So that my steps that day would be guided by God's will rather than my own.
She prepared biscuits for me with hands that had already been overworked,
And served them with the hope that they would empower me to soar.
We ate and went to the fields together to survive another day.
No, I did not rebel against my mama.

I could not rebel against my mama, life was hard enough for her as it was
Being poor and black and female and powerless, her very existence was a struggle.
And in retrospect, she must have been scared to death of every day's unknowns.
The last thing she needed were children who did not love her, honor her, and obey her.
It was enough that she had to endure the indignities of poverty and injustice.
It was enough that she had to spend her nights lonely, deprived, and unfulfilled,
That she had to shelter us, clothe us, and feed us with meager crumbs from leased soil.
So, I did not rebel against my mama.

I could not rebel against my mama,
This woman who birthed me in a ragged house with broken windows and an unfinished floor.
In the November cold she gave me life at the risk of her own life.
And limited her life so that my life might be unlimited—far beyond her imaginations.
She went to work so I could go to school—and did without so I could have.
Many times she went hungry while I ate, and lay awake at night worrying while I soundly slept.
Not once did she weep or complain or give any sign of weakening under her heavy load.
Years later I learned of our poverty—thank God by then I knew of our wealth.

I could not rebel against my mama.
Not this woman who prayed when I was out at night that God would bring me safely home,
And did not sleep until my footsteps on the porch proved that her prayers had been answered once again.
I could not go home at the expense of her prayers and reject the heart that had sent them out.
It was bad enough that I went to bed nightly not knowing of her petitions in my behalf.
It was bad enough that I saw other women's beauty and only her strength,
That I wooed their love and took hers for granted, thanked them, and said nothing to her.
The least I could do was to comply quietly to her few requests.
So, I did not rebel against my mama.

After a hard week's work Mama went to church on Sunday in her white usher's dress.
She took us with her to show the world that we were earthly proud and heavenly bound.
We were her claim to importance and her best hope of deliverance

from her lowly state.

We were God's gift to each other; We to her, and her to us,
Mama introduced us to God early and taught us to honor him in
all of our ways.

We were a team, God, Mama, and us, unwavering, unbeatable,
and inseparable.

Rebelling against Mama for me would have been like rebelling
against God.

So, I could not rebel against my mama.

I could not dampen that smile that she wore through all of our tri-
als and tribulations.

However unbecoming it may have seemed for our situation, she
wore it anyway.

When the hope she placed in her children paid off with their
success, the smile grew brighter.

She was still wearing that bright smile when she went home to be
with Jesus.

Now, just the thought of Mama keeps a smile in my heart, knowing that we are together still, inseparable.

The lessons she taught me, the love she gave to me, and the hope
she left with me, abide.

And have done me so much good that I thank God for her every day.

And I am so glad that I did not rebel against my mama.

We may have passed the time when men are expected to open
doors for women, or give their seats to women, but I hope that we
have not become so modern that women, especially mothers,
don't get some special consideration and respect in our society.
Those who value this quality must keep respect alive.

Rules to Live By

Motherhood

1. Always speak to your mother in a respectful manner.
2. Listen to your mother's advice even if you don't follow it.
3. Never use profanity in the presence of mothers.
4. Within reason, consider your mother's opinion.
5. Honor special days in your mother's life with cards and expressions of appreciation.
6. As your mother ages, make sure she is cared for, especially if your father is not around.
7. Be kind and helpful to any mother and her child/children.
8. Work and vote for a family-friendly society.
9. Live so your mother can brag on you.
10. Call your mother frequently when you move away from home.
11. Develop in your children an appreciation for their grandmother.
12. Take your small children to visit their grand mother.

Family

To make a happy fireside clime to weans and wife,
That's the true pathos and sublime of human life.
—Robert Burns

Many of our values run together and are inseparable. Three of the values that are intrinsically linked are the value we have for mothers, family, and the elderly. Family is the cornerstone of our

society. It is the primary vehicle through which we transmit our culture. It is where we teach new-comers how to grow up and be productive members of society. Just about everything and every-body else in society depend upon the family.

In the last couple of decades we have had a breakdown of the American family, and the value we place on family seems to be declining. Ironically, the decline of the family calls attention to its value.

For the first time since the U. S. Census Bureau started tracking family data, more firstborn children were born out of wedlock in the year 2001 (53 percent) than were born to two parent families. Sixty years ago when the bureau began tracking such data, the figure was 18 percent. There are 10 million single mothers in the U.S. today compared to 3.4 million in 1970. There is definitely a decline in the value we place on family, or at least the kind of family we have traditionally known. There was a time when we thought that every child needed and deserved a stable, two-parent family. Women who got pregnant before they could start such a family often put their children up for adoption in order to have them grow up in stable families. Such was our value for family. Society needs stable families. Many of the social problems that plague America today are traced to the breakdown of the family.

Our definition of family may have changed, the way family life is carried on in the twenty-first century has definitely changed, but Americans still treasure family, and the country, more than ever before, needs stable families.

People of character who value family promote family life and strive to keep families intact. Children should first learn to be good members of their own family. They should be respectful to the head of their households and cooperate and do their fair share to keep the family unit working. Children of good character honor their family name and try to make their parents proud of them. I have never wanted to do anything that would bring shame to my family name. I was fifty-seven years old when my mother died. Upon her death I was able to say that in all of my years my mother had never been awakened in the night by a phone call from the police or had anyone tell her that I had done anything wrong or was ever in trouble. I am still proud of that.

If we value family, good family character dictates that we start families in the right situation, that we not start them before we are ready, and that we not build them on lies and deception. If you are in school and are looking forward to becoming a parent, you should be getting the best education possible so that you can provide for your children the best leadership, advice, and living that your ability allows. You should always be good to young children and you should never mislead a younger child. Once you start a family, good character demands that you always put the needs of your family before your own needs. Few people will respect men or women who selfishly pursue their own interests at the expense of properly taking care of their children.

Rules to Live By

Family

1. Be a good family member at all times.
2. Put family needs before your individual needs.
3. Look after the younger people and seniors in the family.
4. Make time for family activities.
5. Make a special effort to be with family on holidays and special occasions.
6. Get a good education so you can lead and take care of a future family.
7. Be kind to little children.
8. Support family-friendly legislation.
9. Cooperate with family members.
10. Make a genuine attempt to resolve differences with family members.

Respect for the Elderly

As a white candle is to a holy place, so is the beauty of an aged face.
—*Joseph Campbell*

Respect for the elderly is a value of the American people. My age group was taught to have respect for the elderly. During my youth older people in my community were admired and treasured. They were respected and appreciated for their experience, knowledge, and wisdom. The young honored them and benefitted from those attributes.

Today, with so much emphasis being placed on youth and sex appeal, old age is not valued as it once was. Many older adults are abandoned by their children and grandchildren and are left alone at home or in nursing homes with little contact with family members. People who have lived long lives and made contributions to society should be valued and looked out for by others. It appalls me when I hear of scams and fraud directed at the elderly. Every time I hear of an elderly person being abused or taken advantage of, I am left wondering how could someone do such a thing to an old person.

But respect for the elderly has deep roots in American culture. As more Americans live longer our value for the elderly will be tested and I hope strengthened. It is crucial that a society respects its elders, for by doing so, it honors its history and foundation.

Character Component

People of good character who value the elderly respect that stage of life. Each day brings every young person closer to old age. Good character demands that one treat the elderly the way he/she would want to be treated if he were elderly. Just as good character demands that you respect women just because they are women, it demands that you respect the elderly because they are elderly.

The story is told of a young boy who watched his mother take care of his grandmother. Each day when they had their meals the mother would serve the grandmother food in a wooden bowl while she and the son ate from beautiful glass bowls. After watching this for some time the young boy asked his mother why she served his grandmother's food in the wooden bowl. She explained that his grandmother was old and frail and might drop the glass bowl and break it. To avoid risking the loss of a glass bowl, she fed grandmother out of the wooden bowl. After pondering the mother's explanation for a few seconds, the boy then advised his mother to take good care of the wooden bowl. The mother wanted to know why. "So when you're old I can serve you from it," was the son's reply.

Our collective character can be judged by what we allow to happen to the elderly among us and around us. Just as I am angered when I hear of abuse to the elderly, we should all be angry over such things. It is a part of our character to be concerned about the elderly and to show that concern in our actions.

54

Rules to Live By

Respect for the Elderly

1. Be kind to the elderly, starting with those in your own family.
2. Listen politely to the elderly even if you don't take their advice.
3. Never raise your voice in a disrespectful manner to older people.
4. Give the elderly a helping hand, in crossing the street, walking up stairs, etc.
5. Don't rush elderly people.
6. Look out for the elderly by not letting others take advantage of them.
7. Check on the elderly in extreme weather.
8. Shovel elderly people's sidewalks in winter, even if they can't pay you.
9. Don't get upset when elderly people refer to you as boy, girl, or child. To them these are terms of affection.
10. Volunteer at nursing homes.

Taking Personal Responsibility

Today and duty are ours, tomorrow and the results belong to God.
—Victor Hugo

Personal responsibility is to be accountable for your behavior and situation. In a democracy, every adult is ultimately responsible for himself/herself. Regardless of how helpful and supportive

your parents are to you, eventually you will become an adult and will need to take full responsibility for yourself. Adults will respect only those who take that responsibility.

In a free society we have a responsibility to the rest of society not to burden them with the things that we should take care of ourselves. Americans have never liked free loaders. Our spirit of independence demands that we pay our own way.

You should learn to be independent, for as you get older, the respect that you get from the rest of society will be partly determined by how well you take personal responsibility for the things that rightly fall to you. Personal responsibility is essential in a democracy; it is also essential to getting along with others with minimal conflict. The great majority of the social conflicts I have witnessed between adults have involved someone not taking personal responsibility for something he/she should have.

Taking personal responsibility goes far beyond simply taking care of yourself materially. It also means taking responsibility for your behavior by conducting yourself properly and admitting when you have done wrong. In some cases it may mean amending for your wrong with apologies or compensation. Americans don't like people who pass their responsibilities on to others.

People of good character take responsibility for themselves and their actions. They do for themselves the things that are theirs to do, and they seldom pass that responsibility on to others. When they have to turn to others for things, they turn to those with whom they have the appropriate relationship to expect those things. They also make sure that these people are persons for whom they would do similar things.

I try not to get any favors from people for whom I wouldn't do similar favors. I generally don't let people whose lifestyles I disapprove do favors for me. I don't want to be put in the position of having to support activities of theirs of which I do not approve. And I don't want them to be put in the position of doing things for me that I wouldn't do for them. Consequently, I don't ask drug dealers to give me rides to church because I don't want them to ask me to give them rides to the drug house. My getting to church is no more important to them than their getting to the drug house is to me. Character requires that I get my favors from people for whom I would do similar favors if the situation were reversed. And it so often is.

If you have good character and make a mistake, you have to own up to it. You have to do your own chores, do your own homework, and pay your own debts. If you are a young person, you may be tempted to let your parents do more for you than they should, or let others do things for you that they shouldn't, but if you want to be respected as a responsible person, you're going to have to do certain things for yourself. If you don't take personal responsibility you are going to eventually be seen as a bum, not a person of high character.

Rules to Live By

Taking Personal Responsibility

1. Never have others do for you that which you should do for yourself.
2. Know the terms under which persons do things for you.
3. Never turn your duties over to someone else.
4. Do your own homework.
5. Wash your own dishes.
6. Clean your own room.
7. Own up to your mistakes and pay for them if you have to.
8. Write your own "thank you" notes.
9. Make your own apologies.
10. Pay your fair share when eating out with friends.

Diligent and Honest Work

Work keeps at bay three great evils: boredom, vice, and need.
—Voltaire

An honest day's work for an honest day's pay is more than just a slogan; it is a deep conviction. We often identify ourselves according to our work. Carpenter, fireman, policeman, doctor, lawyer, and teacher are titles people proudly wear to indicate the work they do. In America, work is tied to worth. We generally don't think much of people who don't work, especially men.

During some of the toughest times in our country the government started programs to put people to work. Men of character would rather work for their needs than to receive charity. There are people who will not take government assistance such as welfare because they believe that they should work for what they get.

If you are in school, you are probably told that school is your work. In fact, education itself is about work, hard work. In my years in the classroom I found that the students who made the best grades and were the most successful usually had the best work habits. It was true in the classroom, on the sports field, and wherever they congregated. The students who worked were the most successful. In the end, people feel better about themselves when they work for what they get. Your accomplishments will be more appreciated by others if they see evidence that you have worked for them.

Character Component

When you work and carry your own load you exemplify good character. People of good character do not have to be watched on their jobs; they do their work whether they are watched or not. Students who copy their homework from classmates rather than do it themselves demonstrate bad character. Taking credit for work that you didn't do steals credit from the one who did it. Having to be watched on the job is poor character. The people who are most watched on jobs have the smallest salaries. Professional men and women are expected to have the character to do what they agree to do, whether that agreement is verbal or written.

In my profession as a teacher, I definitely needed good character. Teaching is about as close as one can come to being self-employed while having a salary and benefits. Teachers are expected to do their work without being watched and to treat every child fairly regardless of who the child is or what he does. My character was tested by several students over the years, and even more so by their parents. But I always did right by my students. My character and my integrity, and the integrity of the profession were at stake.

If you believe in diligent and honest work your character is shown by the work you do in school, in the home, and on your job. Your willingness or unwillingness to work as you agree is a character statement. When you work in a group good character demands that you do your fair share of the work.

Rules to Live By

Diligent and Honest Work

1. Always put work before play.
2. Finish the jobs that you start.
3. Do your fair share when working in a group.
4. Never take money for work you did not or will not do.
5. Never spend the money paid for a job before the job is done.
6. Charge a fair price for the work you do.
7. Redo jobs that you didn't do right the first time.
8. Take pride in a job well done.
9. Prepare well for the profession you plan to enter.
10. Except in cases of emergency, do not take care of personal matters on your job.

Knowledge

Soon after settling in America, our founding fathers established churches and schools. Both were places where knowledge would be sought and taught. Our first, greatest, and most lasting institutions are institutions of learning. African slaves soon adopted this country's high regard for knowledge. After slavery, the first and most enduring institutions founded by black people were their schools and societies. Across the board, we Americans value knowledge.

To this day, our system of public education is the most accessible in the world. No other nation places the premium on education for all its citizens as does America. We value knowledge for what it has done for our nation and the world.

Our knowledge of agriculture has made us the best fed people on the planet and has enabled us to help feed the world. Our knowledge of science and technology has made us the premiere power of the times. Our schools of medicine attract people from all over the world. More doctors and scientists are trained in the United States than anywhere else on earth. We fund research and exploration at a higher rate than any other nation.

Our space exploration is a quest for knowledge. We explore the seas for more knowledge. We dig deep into caves and explore areas that have been untouched by civilization in a quest for knowledge. We believe that greater knowledge is the key to a better life. Some of our greatest heroes are our thinkers who have left us a legacy of ideas and advancement. Our constitution was drafted by some of the greatest minds of the time. Several of them started schools or had schools named in their honor.

People of good character who value knowledge seek knowledge and support the pursuit of knowledge. Young people of good character apply themselves in school and take full advantage of their country's value for knowledge. They honor their parents' hard work on their jobs by working hard in school.

You exhibit poor character if you use your parents' hard-earned money and don't do your work in school. Parents send kids to school with an unspoken contract: "I'll work and take care of you so you can concentrate on school." Students who don't do their work are breaking a time-honored contract with their parents and their future, and are demonstrating bad character.

People who value learning support institutions of higher learning. Graduates of colleges and universities who have good character show appreciation for the efforts of those who paved the way for them by giving back to those institutions. Parents provide for their children the best education that is available to them. If you value knowledge, your character can be judged by the extent to which you show that value in your daily life. Students of good character who value knowledge use school time wisely. They do their work and respect and appreciate their teachers. They go to school to learn, not just to make good grades. They pursue knowledge in school and on their own. They respect the educational environment, and highly regard their teachers and those who have advanced our knowledge. They become life-long learners.

Rules to Live By

Knowledge

1. Seek to find the facts about issues of interest.
2. Read as much as you can.
3. Listen to those who have knowledge to share with you.
4. Support institutions of learning, especially your own.
5. Respect educators.
6. Apply yourself in school.
7. Support the schools in your neighborhood.
8. Never argue without getting your facts right.
9. Keep up with current events and issues.
10. Be open to new ideas.

Contributing to Society

The more you love, the more you'll find
That life is good and friends are kind.
For only what we give away
Enriches us from day to day.
—Helen Steiner Rice

Americans believe that we all benefit from society and should give something back to society. We are a generous nation, a good and giving people, and we treasure being so. Our heroes have been those who have given of themselves to make the country a better place.

There are literally thousands of organizations and foundations in America that raise and dispense billions of dollars a year to provide materials and services to the less fortunate. These organizations exist and thrive because we believe in contributing to society. We believe that a self-centered life is dishonorable, that it is noble to live for others and not just for one's self. I remember seeing a quotation on the wall of a school I attended as a child that said, "A man wrapped up in himself makes a very small package." I was always encouraged to go beyond myself and think of the larger society.

In my early school years I learned about great Americans like Albert Schweitzer, Harriet Tubman, Mary McLeod Bethune Cookman, Helen Keller, and others who gave back to their society and left a legacy of giving. We were taught that we had a responsibility to give back to the country, starting with our own communities. A life of giving or service was highly valued by my family and my teachers.

Young people today are thought to be selfish. They don't appear to be committed to giving back like their ancestors were. However, giving back to society is still embraced by enough people to make it a prominent value of the American people.

Good character and common decency demand that one give back to those persons and institutions that gave to him. Honorable persons do not wish to be free loaders on society, nor do they want to owe society anything. Therefore, those of good character contribute to society at least to the degree that society contributes to them.

I have always felt that I should make a contribution to my family, my race, my country, and the human family. I don't know who encouraged me to think that way, but it is something I have felt for a long time. I believe in giving back to that which has developed me.

At one point in my teaching career I was sought by a prestigious private school. I refused to take a teaching position with them because having received my education in public schools I felt an obligation to teach in the public schools. I got a good education through the efforts of good and caring people. I was not the best-behaved child, so my teachers had to work a little harder to reach me. As a result, I have given my life to public education and have always tried to help those students who needed a little extra attention. I felt an obligation to give that extra help since my teachers had done it for me.

Selfish adults are not very highly thought of in our society. We tolerate selfishness from children, but as people grow older we expect them to be able to think beyond themselves and include others in their concerns. If you can't do that, you will be seen as a person with bad character. Several month ago while thinking of this subject I expressed my opinion about this matter in a poem:

If I Should Die Today

If I should die today I would owe the world nothing
And it would be far richer because of my stay.
I've never taken more than I have given
And without complaining I've paid my way.
When the world smiled at me I smiled back and more.
When it gave to me I gave back beyond my equal share.
For its kindness I gave a little extra kindness to store
To make up for some future soul with no kindness to spare.
I filled all my days with something good,
And found no time to pursue the bad,
For justice and honor I always stood
And gave each cause the best that I had.
So if I should die today I am at peace.
My slate is clean, my record is clear.
There is no horror of impending decease.
Of a just judgment I have no fear.
We come to this world with no guarantees
And never know how long we will stay.
Our Heavenly Father we should try to please
And make the very best of every day.
I've done the best I could with what I had
And been kind to those who passed my way.
Even though loved ones would be sad
I'd be all right if I would die today.
Every soul should live so well
And be mindful of the shortness of his earthly stay.
And never on evil should you dwell
Because you could die today.
Children of God should be aware
That time is slipping fast
About the things that you have learned to care
Only Godly ones will last.
I spend my time doing Godly things.
They consume my earthly stay.
My soul has been assured heavenly wings
If I should die today.

Young people who want to develop good character around this value can volunteer at hospitals and nursing homes. They can give money to charities and other causes that help people. And they can develop a lifestyle of sharing rather than always wanting to receive.

Rules to Live By

Contributing to Society

1. Give back to the community that gives to you.
2. Volunteer at nursing homes and hospitals.
3. Assist people at your school.
4. Choose a profession that allows you to contribute to society.
5. Give to charitable organizations.
6. Help senior citizens.
7. Donate money to your college.
8. Help young people.
9. Share your knowledge.
10. Practice kindness.

Obeying the Rules

Good order is the foundation of all good things. —*Edmund Burke*

No one is above the rules, and in an orderly society people must obey rules. We are a nation of laws. Our system works only when most of us obey the rules. Whether those rules govern our behavior in the larger society, or our actions on the playground, once they are established, we believe in following them. Playing by the rules is "do unto others as you would have them do unto you" extended to the playground, the work place, and even to relationships. Rules are necessary for order, and only through the adherence to rules can we avoid chaos. Rules govern just about every aspect of our lives. They are for our good and we benefit from obeying them. The order and safety of our society depend

upon people obeying the rules. If drivers did not obey traffic rules, driving would be chaotic and deadly.

Practically all of our interactions are governed by rules that must be followed by the great majority of the people in order for those interactions to be successful. Our civility as a nation can be measured by the degree to which most of us obey the rules.

One's character can be judged by how closely he obeys the just rules that govern his behavior in any particular situation. Since we benefit from others obeying the rules good character demands that we obey them also. To ask others to obey rules that we will not obey is bad character.

Many school activities give you a chance to test or build your character. Many activities are done in groups, and in practically all group settings there are rules and regulations. When you abide by the rules while working with a group, you develop character. Playing by the rules is what you give back to the group for being allowed to be a part of the group.

Playing by the rules earns us a right to play with others who are playing by the rules. When we choose to interact within a group we enter into a social contract with the others who are in that group to abide by the rules. To enter the contract and not abide by the rules is bad character. People of good character learn the rules before they get involved in an interaction, and once they sign off on the rules they play by them, even when it hurts. Children who learn to play by the rules when they are young usually grow up to be law-abiding citizens. Young people who are allowed to break the rules often wind up in and out of trouble with the law.

There will be rules in sports, friendships, households, and marriages. Those who learn to play by the rules prepare themselves to get along better and be more respected in each of those situations.

Good character demands that you obey the rules even when no one is watching. However, in many cases, people are watching even when you think they are not.

Rules to Live By

Obeying the Rules

1. Know what the rules are.
2. Obey the rules or don't get involved.
3. Demand that others obey the rules.
4. Accept the penalty when you break the rules.
5. Make sure that the rules you make are fair.
6. Don't have one set of rules for yourself and another set for others if all other things are equal.
7. Don't get angry with people for enforcing just rules.
8. Don't claim ignorance of a rule after you've broken it.

Respect for Authority

All authority belongs to the people. *—Thomas Jefferson*

Since we are a nation of laws or rules it is absolutely imperative that those who enforce those rules are obeyed and respected. Therefore, we value respect for authority and authority figures. Respect for authority is to give the proper submission and honor to authority and authority figures. It is to  give to them the compliance and cooperation that is appropriate for their rank. Even when we think that the person in the position of authority does not deserve our respect, we respect the authority vested in the position itself. Respect for authority is essential to our civility and stability.

Of the values discussed in this book, respect for authority is probably the one that is most lacking in young people today. Young Americans don't hold the same respect for authority and authority figures as do older Americans. When I talk with teachers and administrators at the schools I visit, they tell me that the biggest problem they have with today's students is their lack of respect for authority. There has been a tremendous decline in such respect the last couple of decades.

Since ours is a representative government, a high respect for authority and authority figures is necessary. Those who are in positions of authority are usually placed there by the rest of us. To disrespect them is to disrespect our society and our system. Authority is the combined will of our people vested in and represented by those in positions of authority. We have always valued respecting those persons and positions. And even though the value is now in decline it is still one of the cherished values of the American people.

Those who would have good character and value respecting authority must themselves respect authority. Each of us benefits from people exercising authority responsibly. The checks and balances of our system work only when authority is respected. I saw a splendid and dramatic example of how respecting authority is fundamental to our peace and stability in 1962.

That was the year that James Meredith, a black student, enrolled at the University of Mississippi at Oxford. The Governor of the state vowed to keep him out of that all-white university and called on the state's National Guard to help him block Meredith's entrance. The governor was in authority over the state's National Guard. But our constitution places the federal government in authority over the state government. The Supreme Court, our ultimate legal authority, had ruled that black students could go to any public school in the country, and those schools in Mississippi were not excluded. So President Kennedy nationalized the Mississippi National Guard, placing them under his authority. He then sent an additional 30,000 federal troops to the university to protect James Meredith's entrance into it. Ultimately, the people in Mississippi, even though many of them were very much against a black student attending Ole Miss, relented and respected the ultimate authority of the country that was vested in the president.

Respect for authority is easier to maintain when people in positions of authority exercise their authority with respect and restraint. If you ever want to be in a position of authority, you should respect those who are placed over you so that when you are placed over others you will know what it is like to have someone in authority over you. People who know what it is like to be subjected to authority are more likely to treat those they have authority over with respect and dignity. It is bad character to disrespect authority and then seek positions of authority. Since education prepares people to exercise authority, honorable people seeking education should respect authority.

Most of us benefit from the country's respect for authority, for most of us have been, or will be under somebody's authority. And most of us will at some point in our lives be in authority over something or someone. Some young people think it is cool to be anti-authority and anti-system, but our society depends upon the great majority of us supporting the rules and supporting those who enforce the rules. We all benefit from an orderly society and, therefore, should contribute to that order by respecting authority and obeying the just rules that govern us. Good character demands that we do so.

Rules to Live By

Respect for Authority

1. Always follow the rules or guidelines.
2. Give appropriate respect to those in charge.
3. Defer to authority figures to the appropriate degree.
4. Don't give rules that you would not obey.
5. Do not seek authority in areas that you do not respect authority.
6. Do not abuse authority.
7. Exercise authority with dignity and respect.
8. Never pass the buck with your authority.
9. Be humble in your exercise of authority.
10. Never accept positions of authority that you don't intend to carry out.

Preserving the Planet (Conservation)

Nature never did betray the heart that loved her.
—William Wordsworth

Taking care of the planet has become very important to us. We should all share the responsibility of taking care of the planet. This planet does not belong to any of us, but is shared by all of us. Those who came before us passed it on to us, and we should pass it on to those who follow us as well preserved as we found it. Unnecessary pollution, careless destruction of vegetation, wanton and useless destruction of wild life are unacceptable.

We have not always honored our responsibility for the planet. In years past conservation was not nearly as popular as it is today. Indians were portrayed as people who valued the planet, while the rest of us were seen as polluters. But during the fifties and sixties we became aware of the harm we were doing through our pollution and waste and developed a new concern about the planet. Groups such as Green Peace, and observances such as Earth Day, remind us of the importance of taking care of the planet. Taking care of the earth should be viewed in the same way that one views taking care of his house; both are his dwelling places.

The value of taking care of the planet is one that is embraced more strongly by young Americans than by older Americans. I think that a greater awareness of the harm we were doing to our environment in the past has brought about a greater concern among our young people for its upkeep. It is natural that younger people would be more concerned about the upkeep of the planet since they are likely to have more time left to live on it.

If you shared a house with someone you would be expected to take responsibility for keeping the house clean and making it last as long as it could. If you didn't fulfill your responsibility of keeping the house clean and preserving it, you would be seen as a bad house partner and probably wouldn't be wanted there. If you insisted on staying and refusing to do your part in helping keep the house suitable for living, you would probably be called a bad character, along with some other names.

The earth is much bigger than a house, but it is still our home. The character of those who value the planet can be judged by how well they take care of it. We can not be held accountable for things that we didn't know, but now that we know how to take better care of the planet, people of good character should do so.

Those who came before us, to the best of their knowledge, kept the earth in good shape for us. We owe it to those who will follow us to pass on to them an earth that is at least as good as it was when we inherited it. Civilized people take care of their dwelling places. Conservation, recycling, keeping your neighborhood clean, and encouraging others to do the same are ways of taking care of the planet.

Today's youth are brought up knowing the importance of the environment and have been constantly reminded of the need to take care of it. Therefore, if you do not do your part to preserve the planet, that is definitely a show of bad character.

Rules to Live By
Preserving the Planet (Conservation)

1. Don't litter.
2. Don't pollute the air or water.
3. Respect animal life and habitation areas.
4. Don't kill animals for sport.
5. Protect the rain forest.
6. Be responsible in the forest (don't cause forest fires).
7. Don't waste resources.
8. Don't dispense chemicals into the environment (car motor oil, etc.).
9. Car pool when possible.
10. Don't smoke in public places.

Gratitude

Thanksgiving for a former, invites God to bestow a second benefit.
—Robert Herrick

One of the first words I was taught after "Mama" and "Daddy" was "tartar." I have no idea of its origin, or how it is spelled. "Tartar" is the word that black people taught their children to express gratitude before they could form the sounds for "thank you." So, in a sense, these children learned to be thankful before they learned how to talk. Gratitude is a strong value in this country. We are a grateful people and that gratitude runs deep in our culture. Gratitude is the feeling of indebtedness, the belief that a force or forces outside of yourself have positively impacted your situation or condition. In other words, things are a little better for you than you could have made them all by yourself. It is also a recognition that things could almost always be worse than they are.

Gratitude is rooted in the belief that no one should or can take full credit for the positive things about his life outcome; therefore, we should all be grateful that things are as good for us as they are. Our notion of gratitude is partly rooted in the great advantage we have of being Americans. Our country is vast and rich with natural resources. It is protected on all sides by natural borders and friendly neighbors. We have wealth, power, prestige, ingenuity, and seemingly unlimited possibilities. Since our situation is better than we could have planned it, we think that a natural response to our good fortune should be gratitude. We value gratitude and don't care much for ungrateful people.

Judging one's character on the basis of gratitude can be difficult. So when it comes to gratitude, you have to be the judge of your own character. There are observable things that grateful people do that will indicate their gratitude. If their gratitude is rooted in their religious beliefs, they usually say prayers of thanksgiving and follow the teachings that their religion prescribes for grateful people. They sometimes show their gratitude by sharing with others. Gratitude and selfishness don't fit very well together. Most of the people I've known who expressed great gratitude were also caring and giving people. They didn't hesitate to share what they called their "blessings" with others.

I think the best indications of one's gratitude is his/her giving and humility. Since gratitude is rooted in the feeling that what you have came partly from forces outside of yourself, to be arrogant and boastful about your accomplishments is not a show of gratitude. If you take all of the credit for something you can not be sufficiently grateful for it. So if you want to show good character around the value of gratitude, keep in mind that people will expect you to be humble and to share. However, whether you really are grateful, and to what extent, can never be really known by others. They can only judge by your behavior.

Rules to Live By

Gratitude

1. Always express thanks for favors you receive.
2. Never act as if people have to do anything for you, or even be nice to you.
3. Share with those who have less.
4. Acknowledge the contributions that others make to your life.
5. Write thank-you notes for special favors and gifts.

Humility

Get someone else to blow your horn and the sound will carry twice as far. —*Will Rogers*

Along with gratitude, and partly an indication of it, is humility. We value humility. Humility is meekness of spirit, the acceptance that one is on an equal plane with the rest of humanity, no better or no worse. Americans have never liked arrogant or boastful people. Arrogance sends a message that people think too highly of themselves. When people think too highly of themselves it is often at the expense of thinking too little of others. Humility is important to Americans because here people are not above the law, they are not above others, and they are not above respecting the values of society. We value humility and like to see it displayed in the highest of places. We want to see humility in our leaders. We want to see it in our great athletes, even after their greatest triumphs. We are much more tolerant of arrogance in people in low stations in life than we are in people in high positions. In Shakespeare's play "Julius Caesar," it was said to be the fear of the lack of humility in Julius Caesar that caused the conspirators, especially Brutus, to kill him. Throughout the literary history of the Western world arrogance has been warned against and humility has been admired. The appreciation of humility is deeply rooted in our culture. It is a value that we still hold today.

If one is humble and has good character he can never be boastful or indignant toward others. Humble people of good character must always show the proper respect for others and their positions. They must obey authority and respect authority figures. Humble people respect the elderly.

If you are to display humility, you must do so in victory as well as in defeat. One of the things I admired about the great basketball player, Julius Erving, was his humility in both defeat and victory. He was never an "in your face" player. He respected his opponents, even though he was better than most of them. He let his performance tell the story. His performance told that story more eloquently than his words ever could have. If you are an athlete, good character demands that you practice good sportsmanship and show respect to your teammates and opponents, regardless of your talent or performance level. If you are smarter than others, better looking than others, richer than others, or just have had better breaks in life than others, you are not to let any of those advantages cause you to act as if you are actually better than they are. There is a stanza from Rudyard Kipling's poem "If" that is quite appropriate here.

> If you can talk with crowds and keep your virtue,
> Or walk with kings nor lose the common touch:
> If neither foes nor loving friends can hurt you;
> If all men count with you but, none too much
> If you fill the unforgiving minute
> With sixty seconds worth of distance run—
> Yours is the earth and everything that's in it
> And which is more, you'll be a man, my son!

As you can tell by the ending, the poem was addressed to young men. Its message here is intended for young women as well. Humility is a desirable quality for anyone who wants good character.

Rules to Live By

Humility

1. Never take great credit for your good fortune.
2. Don't brag on your accomplishments.
3. Don't carry on about yourself in the presence of others.
4. Wait your turn to do things or to speak in groups.
5. Don't belittle other people.
6. Don't gloat in victory.
7. Don't become too depressed over defeat. (You're not too good to lose.)
8. Acknowledge others' contributions to your life.
9. Don't monopolize conversations.
10. Don't constantly remind people of the things you do better than they do them.

Loyalty

I only regret that I have but one life to lose for my country.
—*Nathan Hale*

Loyalty is devotion and commitment that are sustained through changing fortunes and circumstances. We value loyalty to our beliefs, families, friends, country, to our institutions, and to those who are loyal to us. Loyalty is a great quality and it is understandable that a great country would value it. The success of our country and institutions depends upon our loyalty to them. Our country depends upon loyalty from the citizenry. Employers expect loyalty from workers and workers expect loyalty from their companies. Friendships are strengthened through loyalty and family ties are built around loyalty. Loyalty is a beautiful and powerful characteristic. However, it can be painful and ugly when people give loyalty and do not receive it in return. People who are loyal to companies, friends, and families, only to have those entities fail them when they need them most are often devastated. Because betrayal is so unpleasant to Americans, we value loyalty and look with disdain upon those who betray loyalties.

Individuals of good character who want loyalty must give it. Our character can be judged by how devoted we are to those who are devoted to us. I heard a story about an incident that occurred during the Viet Nam War. It is said that the enemy attacked a group of American soldiers, killing some and wounding several others. The unit had to retreat to safety. One soldier, after finding cover, discovered that his closest friend was not with the group. He wanted to return and look for his friend, but the captain told the soldier that his friend had been hit by enemy fire and was probably dead. And even if he were alive, he couldn't risk losing another life trying to save someone who was probably going to die anyway.

After hearing the Captain's gloomy assessment, this friend ran back through a hail of gunfire to the place where they had left his wounded buddy. Upon finding his friend near death, he stayed with him until he died. He then ran back through the gunfire to rejoin his group. When he got back to the other soldiers, badly wounded and bleeding, his captain reminded him that he had told him not to go, and that not only did he not save his friend, but he himself had been wounded and could die. He then asked the wounded soldier if going back to get his friend was worth risking his own life. The soldier assured his captain that it was worth it. He said his friend had whispered to him with his dying breath, "I knew you would come." This soldier was loyal to the end.

Loyalty is a character test for those who believe in it and benefit from it. In these days, however, one must be very careful about to whom and what he gives his devotion. If you devote yourself to the wrong people and causes, that loyalty could easily hurt you. So choose well the people and things to which you give your devotion. After you make the choice your character will be judged by the strength of that devotion.

Rules to Live By

Loyalty

1. Be as good to others as they are to you.
2. Express appreciation for loyalty.
3. Reward loyalty.
4. Keep secrets that you promise to keep (except when you would betray a higher loyalty).
5. Never kiss and tell.
6. Always return favors.
7. Be true to your beliefs.
8. Be consistent.
9. Be good to your parents.
10. Support your teams, win or lose.

Compassion

What does love look like? It has the hands to help others. It has the feet to hasten to the poor and needy. It has the eyes to see misery and want. It has the ears to hear sighs and sorrows. That is what love looks like. —*St. Augustine*

Compassion is the general concern we have for others. It is caring about others and their situation. It is the sympathy one shows for suffering and pain. Our compassion is rooted in the belief that at some level we should feel each other's pain. We value compassion and are afraid of people who have no compassion. Just as we want our leaders to have humility, we also want them to have compassion. We are afraid to put people in power who have no compassion. When I consider whether a person would be a good teacher, or good with children in any capacity, I look at the person's capacity for compassion. Some people have a greater capacity for compassion than do others, but we Americans want to see some compassion in everybody. We don't like, or even understand, people who show no compassion.

Because we value compassion, we find it difficult to understand serial killers and mass murderers, and people who are willing to kill hundreds and even thousands of innocent people to make political points. Americans see compassion as natural to the human condition. Not to have it strikes us as being non-human or inhumane. We admire people who show compassion and dislike those who can not be moved to care. We even value showing compassion toward animals.

Ultimately, none of us can match the forces that life will throw at us. At some point we will need the sympathy of others to endure. We all need and receive compassion and should give it when appropriate.

Character Component

People with good character demonstrate their compassion through showing concern for others, especially those who are less fortunate. Compassionate people are sensitive to the needs of others. They understand that we will always be surrounded by people who are less fortunate who will need the compassion and care of others. Compassionate people look after the weak and feeble, the sick and suffering, and the poor and downtrodden. Good character demands that we show compassion when we are in positions to do so. Regardless of your station in life you will likely, at some point, have an opportunity to show compassion. You can show compassion to a co-worker, a classmate, a teacher, a competitor, or even a stranger. A show of compassion often leaves a lasting impression on people. Not to show it when it is appropriate will also leave a lasting memory.

I experienced many memorable moments in and out of the classroom with my students. Those that stand out were often displays of compassion. One in particular happened after the death of one of my brothers. I didn't tell my students about my brother's death. However, a few of them did find out about it. On the afternoon that I was to leave for the funeral one of my students stayed after class and gave me a sympathy card from him and his parents. He told me that he had heard about my brother's death and he and his family wanted me to know that my family and I were in their thoughts and prayers.

I must have taught some great lessons that semester, and had some great responses from my students. But what I remember most was that child coming to his teacher at a time when I was dealing with death, the common foe of us all, and saying, "We feel for you in this ordeal and we hope you come through it just fine." He showed great character, and the fact that I remember it should indicate what it did for me.

Rules to Live By

Compassion

1. Help those who are less fortunate.
2. Look out for young people and senior citizens.
3. Always give people credit for doing their best, even when it is not enough.
4. Be kind to people who are suffering, even those you don't like.
5. Forgive infractions.
6. Listen to people when they need to talk.
7. Temper justice with mercy.
8. Sympathize with people of different races and cultures.
9. Forgive debts for people who can not repay you.
10. Don't gloat in victory.

Worthy Accomplishments

The way to be nothing is to do nothing. —*Nathaniel Howe*

Americans expect people to do something worthwhile with their lives. We value people who accomplish things. A good life should be one of worthy accomplishments. Worthy accomplishment once meant achieving something that was valuable to society as well as to oneself. Benjamin Franklin is a great example of valuing worthy accomplishments. His life was lived in the pursuit of worthy accomplishments. Our country has benefited greatly from his efforts and the efforts of others who believed that we should pursue worthy accomplishments.

Worthy accomplishment was certainly valued in my family when I was growing up, as it was in most families at that time. We often heard the phrase, "Make something of yourself." The people whom we held in esteem were those who had made something of themselves. Making something of yourself did not mean that you had to be great, it simply meant that you had to improve upon the circumstances of your birth. In fact, each generation was to be a bit better than the generation that had preceded it.

My family did not just want my siblings and me to be successful, they wanted us to be successful at something that was worthy, like teaching, the ministry, medicine, farming, or some enterprise that was highly regarded and valuable to society. Those of us who were fortunate enough to graduate from high school or go to college had to be something that was really distinguished and valuable to society. It was slothful not to work hard and make something of yourself. To be respectable, everyone had to do something worthwhile with his/her life.

To value worthy accomplishments is to be about the business of working toward those accomplishments. People of good character work toward the things they want. To proclaim it and not work to claim it is bad character. Students who claim they want an education but will not work to achieve it show bad character. Work builds character. Working toward honorable goals for yourself and your society builds strong character.

If you believe in worthy accomplishments and would have good character you must strive to be those things that you have been given the natural ability to be. You can not settle for being a nurse if you have the ability and the opportunity to be a doctor. If you believe in this value, good character requires that you aim as high as you can and be the very best that you can be. I am discouraged that so many bright kids want to be athletes and entertainers because those professions are glamorous and pay a lot of money. For people of good character, money and glamour should not be the main considerations in choosing a profession.

My students were always amazed when I told them that I turned down an opportunity to play major league baseball because I wanted to be a minister and college professor. They couldn't imagine anyone turning down the chance to make that much money to do something that they thought they were better suited for and that society was more in need of. But I did. I am not suggesting that you should not be a professional athlete or entertainer if you feel that such is your life's calling and you have the talent and opportunity to do so. I am simply saying that good character demands that we be what we are truly cut out to be if we can make a decent living doing that. It is a tough call, but good character sometimes demands tough choices. Whatever your talent is, if you have good character, you have to get up and do something worthwhile.

Rules to Live By

Worthy Accomplishments

1. Keep an immediate and long-range goal at all times.
2. Do your best at whatever you attempt.
3. Never be jealous of others' accomplishments.
4. Never boast about your accomplishments.
5. Be satisfied when you have done your best.
6. Pursue goals that are good for others as well as yourself.
7. Pursue honorable goals honorably.
8. Work hard to accomplish your goals.
9. Make sacrifices for your goals.
10. Share your success with others.

Honesty and Integrity

No legacy is so rich as honesty. —*William Shakespeare*

We value truth. I remember reading a story as a fourth grader about George Washington cutting down a cherry tree and refusing to lie about it. My teachers and parents stressed being truthful. We Americans think that it is sometimes worse to lie about a bad thing than to actually do a bad thing. Many people in high places have gotten into more trouble about lying about their bad deeds than from committing them. Many parents teach their children to always tell the truth even when it hurts. Liars have been despised in our culture as far back as biblical days. Truth and honesty go together.  It is dishonest to lie. We value honesty in speech and behavior. Truthfulness is a criterion by which just about anyone can be judged, while lying is an indication of many other character faults.

During my youth I often heard people say, "If you lie you will steal." I never knew why they thought that lying was an indication of thievery. I finally realized that they deduced that stealing is dishonest; so is lying. If you do one, they assumed you would do the other. Just as a doctor can look into a patient's eyes and detect faults with his health, one can look into one's speech and detect faults with his character. Therefore, Americans have valued honesty in speech.

In the end, honesty is the ultimate test of one's character. Whatever a person believes, whatever a person espouses, whatever a person is, his character can be judged by the way in which his life reflects those beliefs. And isn't that what character is? When it is all summed up, character is honesty. Remember that statement by Socrates that I quoted earlier in this book: **"The shortest and surest way to live with honor in the world, is to be in reality what we would appear to be; all human virtues increase and strengthen themselves by the practice and experience of them."**

Character is an honest portrayal in one's life of what he claims is in his heart. It is "walking the talk." It is the extent to which he is what he says he is. If one values his word, when he gives it he tries to keep it. I want to share with you a story from my book, *A Little Book For Big People.* It comes from the chapter "Turning Mistakes into Breaks."

Years ago in a rural community in Mississippi there was a gentleman whose name was John. John was a rather nice man but he was a drunk. His wife was a devoted churchgoer. But John never went to church. During an October month many years ago the church his wife belonged to was having a revival. They had an out of town evangelist and the whole community was talking about the revival. Each night the church was packed. On Wednesday night when the preacher finished his sermon and extended an invitation to the unchurched to accept Christ, in walked John, the drunk. Everybody in the church was surprised. Some of them were embarrassed, if not for themselves, for his wife. John was drunk. The smell of whiskey was on him. The preacher looked up and saw John heading down the aisle and reached out his hand to him. "Come," said the preacher, "and give your life to Christ." Since the preacher was not from that community he had no way of knowing that John was the local drunk.

John walked right down the aisle and gave his hand to the preacher. The preacher asked him did he believe that Jesus Christ would save him in a dying hour. John told the preacher that he believed so. The preacher asked John did he want to be baptized. He assured the preacher that he did. So the preacher took John into the church, even though he was drunk. John's wife was terribly embarrassed; she left the church in tears. John went home after church and fell asleep.

The next morning one of the deacons from the church stopped by to see John who was just waking up from his drunken stupor. The deacon told John how embarrassed they all had been when he had come to the revival the previous night drunk and joined the church. John protested to the deacon that he had done no such thing. The deacon assured him that he had. His wife joined in and told him what a fool he had made of himself, and how he had embarrassed her. John sat at the table and had the deacon go over in specific details what he had done. The deacon told him that he had indeed marched into the church at the end of the sermon and told the preacher that he was accepting Christ and wanted to be baptized. "Is that what I said?" asked John. "Yes," replied the deacon. "That is what you said, and the whole community is talking about it. They say you ought to be ashamed of yourself, playing with God like that." John sat at the table and thought about what the deacon had said. He had made a great mistake. He was a drunk, but he was not one to play with the Lord.

That evening the revival continued. As the choir sang before the preacher preached, John walked in the door. This time he did not smell like whiskey. He had a clean shave, clean clothes, an ironed shirt, and his hair was neatly combed. He took a seat in the middle of the church. Everybody's eyes were fixed on him as the service went on. The preacher preached a strong sermon. When he finished and extended an invitation to join the church, John got up and walked down to the preacher. When the church got quiet he spoke. He told the preacher that the people had told him what had happened the night before. He said that they had told him that he had come down the aisle and given the preacher his hand and given his life to Christ. The preacher assured him that that is what he had done. John gave his hand to the preacher again and said, "If that is what I said, then that is what I had better do. When can I be baptized?" John was baptized the following Sunday. He never took another drink and he became one of the most faithful Christians that community had ever known. He became a deacon of the church and served in that position until the day he died.

Even though this man was the neighborhood drunk he had character. And when he found out that he had given his word to a minister in front of a congregation of people, he decided he needed to honor his word. He needed to be what he said he was. Once he accepted the challenge, he was true to his confession for the rest of his life. Honesty is the ultimate test of character. Everything else hinges on it.

If a person is really honest, he will treat others the way he wishes to be treated, he will play by the rules, give a day's work for a day's pay, and give back to that which has given to him. If a person is honest he will protect the environment that has been preserved for him and will pay his own way in the world. If a person is honest he will give loyalty where he has received it and tell the truth and do the right thing.

In the end, the test of character is honesty. Character is the degree to which one's behavior mirrors his beliefs. If one is truly honest, what you see is always what you will get. The degree to which a person demonstrates honesty is the degree to which his character can be judged as good or bad.

Rules to Live By

Honesty and Integrity

1. Be what you claim to be.
2. Speak the truth always.
3. Return favors.
4. Pay your bills.
5. Take the blame for your blunders.
6. Do a day's work for a day's pay.
7. Don't accept favors that you wouldn't give.
8. Keep secrets that you promise to keep.
9. Do what you promise people you will do.
10. Admit when you are lost.

Courage

Courage is a quality so necessary for maintaining virtue, that it is always respected, even when it is associated with vice.
—Samuel Johnson

We value courage. The people whom we most admire in American history and even in western cul-ture are those who displayed courage and did not let their fears deter them from their pursuits. Courage is defined in the diction-ary as mental or moral strength to venture, persevere, and withstand danger, fear, or difficulty.

Courage is not the absence of fear, but rather the commitment to an outcome that is stronger than the fears that stand between you and that outcome. In fact, there can be no courage if there is no fear. Courage is measured in proportion to the fears it confronts. Courage is highly valued in America.

At a very early age American children are taught to confront their fears, to develop courage. The very first thing I can remember doing to confront my fears was to sleep with the light off, to face the darkness. It was common practice when I was young that if a child fell from a horse or a bike, he was to get right back on it and ride before his fears mounted and rendered him too scared to ever ride again.

Courage is highly valued by Americans because many of our other values depend upon our having the courage to embrace and maintain them. As Robert Louis Stevenson said, "Courage, the footstool of the virtues upon which they stand." Acquiring and keeping what we have in America is a constant struggle against the forces that oppose us and our values. Our current fight against terrorism is an ever present reminder of the courage necessary to maintain our freedoms and openness. We accept that challenge.

One of the reasons I feel such a sense of appreciation for those who serve in our Armed Forces is because of the courage they show daily in their defense of our freedoms. But not only in them is courage seen, but in the lives of ordinary people as they courageously confront their fears, obstacles, and challenges and triumph over them. This courage is seen in our police officers, fire fighters, postal workers, educators, and millions of our ordinary citizens bravely facing their challenges every day to keep this country working. You see courage in your parents, classmates, team mates, and even in yourself as you surmount your fears and pursue your goals. Americans admire courage.

Character Component

Those who value courage must not shrink from a task simply because there are risks involved, and they should never put others up to take risks that they themselves would not take. People of character who value courage can not take the safe road, the easy road, or the sure road. Courage requires you to venture out and confront your fears and your doubts. Courage requires that if there is something good and worthwhile that you want to do, but think you might fail at it, or be laughed at for doing it, that you do it anyway. If there is something that you believe in and want to stand up for, but some people who disagree may turn against you if you do, courage requires that you take your stand. Sometimes you will stand almost alone, but if it is the courageous thing to do, that is what courage requires. If there is a girl/boy you want to talk to but think you might be rejected, you have to make your move anyway and risk rejection. Courageous people do not choose things because they are popular or easy. It takes courage to take the last shot in the basketball game when the game is on the line. It takes courage to try a field goal with three seconds on the clock and your team is behind by two points. But you must confront your fears if you are to be a person of courage.

However, courage is not foolish chance taking, but the ability to confront that which is difficult, dangerous, and even that at which one is unlikely to succeed. Driving under the influence of alcohol is not courageous, it is stupid, illegal, and could get you killed. And it's bad character. Playing a sport while hurt is not courageous unless it is simply a matter of enduring the pain, and not a possibility of further damaging the injury and jeopardizing your future health. Doing something wrong or illegal to be accepted into a group might be courageous, but it is a poor use of a great

103

attribute. Courage is most admired when it is used to pursue noble outcomes. For people of good character, the courageous thing to do is also the right thing to do.

Rules to Live By

Courage

1. Stand up for what you believe though it may be unpopular.
2. Be willing to take the consequences of your stance.
3. Don't pass the buck when the going gets tough.
4. Don't do foolish things to show courage.
5. Speak up in class even though your answer might be wrong.
6. Express your feelings honestly even though you might be rejected.
7. If at first you don't succeed, keep trying.
8. Don't dwell on the worst thing that could happen to you.
9. Try new ventures: sports, hobbies, travels, and meeting new friends.
10. Don't use your courage to do illegal or bad things.

Virtue

Virtue is a kind of beauty, health, and good habit of the soul.
—Plato

Virtue is a word that you have probably not heard very often. You might not even know what it means. But virtue has been a tremendous value in American culture and western civilization for a long time. The Greek philosophers extolled and pursued virtue. There has been a high value on the virtuous life throughout western civilization. So what is virtue? Virtue is the embodiment of a cluster of the values that we cherish. It is a physical representation of our ideal of goodness. A virtuous person is one who has elevated character to its highest state. He/she has become what the rest of us aspire to be, and admire seeing in others. The desire of good people is to be virtuous. Virtue is the crossroad where religion, education, and philosophy meet. At the end of the day, the aim of education is virtue. When all is said and done, the aim of religion is virtue. After ideas have been endlessly examined, the aim of philosophy is virtue. In the end, for noble people, the aim of all knowledge is virtue, to put one's actions in line with the laws of the universe, whether they are physical, social, or spiritual.

In a noble society virtue is valued above wealth, fame, power, prestige, and popularity. In a noble society virtue is all of these things and more. You may seek importance by pursuing fame, wealth, and popularity—sometimes through unethical and devious means. And in today's climate, it often works. But I remember a time (as you may say, back in the day) when the most highly honored persons were those whose lives best embodied the values of the community.

Today we have seemingly strayed from those values. It is assumed that young people today are not interested in being virtuous, but are interested mainly in material things: popularity, cheap fame and glory, and an easy life. But as you think abut the people you most admire, you may discover that you, too, are impressed with virtue.

Character Component

If you desire to be virtuous, it is a great desire. You are setting a high standard for yourself, for the character of a virtuous person must be above reproach. Even the appearance of impropriety is bad for a virtuous person. A virtuous person must be an example of many of the values we cherish. Not only must his commitment to his values be strong, but the values themselves must be good and in the proper order of priority. A virtuous person must be slow to anger. She must hold her tongue when others would lash out. She must walk away when others would engage in fruitless fights. He must pick up the paper from the classroom floor even though he didn't put it there. He must stay after practice and gather up the equipment even though it was not his responsibility. She must not complain when she is wrongly accused, especially when the accusation is sincere and the punishment is not harsh. A virtuous person must be patient with the weak and compassionate with those who are suffering. She must be responsible in her behavior, and moderate in her appetite. He must be even-tempered; not given to extremes of any sort. A virtuous person must not engage in meaningless chatter and shall not gossip or repeat questionable information that could bring harm to the innocent. A virtuous person is consistent for she lives by principles that vary little through changing times and fortunes. A virtuous person is humble. He does not boast of his goodness or good fortune, and he works to make the world a better place.

Rules to Live By

Virtue

1. Always speak the truth.
2. Give your best toward every worthwhile effort.
3. Always take the lead in noble ventures.
4. Be a friend to the elderly, women and children.
5. Forgive easily.
6. Apologize without reservation.
7. Sympathize with others' weaknesses.
8. Earn your living doing honorable work.
9. Live in harmony with your religion and/or philosophy.
10. Look after your parents.
11. Help family members when they need help.
12. Spend time with nieces and nephews.
13. Always speak encouraging words to others.
14. Show compassion for others, even those of other races and nations.
15. Champion the underdog.
16. Win and lose gracefully.
17. Never be vindictive.
18. Never do anything to the extreme.
19. Don't complain.
20. Be courageous in the face of danger.

Test Your Character

Now that you have read through these twenty-five values I hope that you have a better understanding of values and the role they play in character development. I also hope that you have a better understanding of this country and the things we value, and consequently, a better understanding of yourself and the things you value. Most of your time and money will be spent pursuing the things that you value, which is why your values have so much influence in determining what you become.

In the introduction of this book I told you that you are in the process of becoming what you will one day become. Hopefully, you are becoming a person of great character, and your character will be developed through the commitment to good values. Now that you have read this book and these values have been called to your attention, I wonder how many of them can you recognize in your own value system, and how committed are you to them. I have composed a test to get at those answers. The test is for fun, but it might be a pretty good indication of what kind of person you are becoming, especially when these values are used as a measure. Let's take the test. Follow these instructions:

Grade yourself on each of the twenty-five values on a scale of 1-10 based upon your commitment to the value, and how much your behavior reflects that commitment. Remember, values plus commitment equal character. Ten is the highest level of commitment, which means that your commitment to that value is very strong and your behavior is perfectly aligned with your beliefs. If you are not a ten, and few of us are, you move down the scale to a 9, 8, 7, until you find the number that best represents your belief in and commitment to that value. If you do not think that a particular value is important and you do not try to act on it in any way, give yourself a 0 for it. Now go to the values and circle the number that best represents your belief in, and commitment to, each one. Once you have scored yourself on each of the twenty-five values, add your scores and place the combined score on the line provided. That is your character score. (This is an open book test, you can go back and review the values as you take the test.)

10. Exceptional   **9.** Outstanding   **8.** Good

7. Above average   **6.** Average   **5.** Below average

4. Weak   **3-0** Not in evidence

Circle the number that best represents your embracing of the value.

Life and human dignity
1   2   3   4   5   6   7   8   9   10

Religion and religious freedom
1   2   3   4   5   6   7   8   9   10

Our country and citizenship
1   2   3   4   5   6   7   8   9   10

Personal freedoms
1   2   3   4   5   6   7   8   9   10

Respect for the rights of others
1   2   3   4   5   6   7   8   9   10

Respect for others' property

1   2   3   4   5   6   7   8   9   10

Justice and fair play

1   2   3   4   5   6   7   8   9   10

Motherhood

1   2   3   4   5   6   7   8   9   10

Family

1   2   3   4   5   6   7   8   9   10

Respect for the elderly

1   2   3   4   5   6   7   8   9   10

Taking personal responsibility

1   2   3   4   5   6   7   8   9   10

Diligent and honest work

1   2   3   4   5   6   7   8   9   10

Knowledge

1   2   3   4   5   6   7   8   9   10

Contributing to society

1   2   3   4   5   6   7   8   9   10

Obeying the rules

1   2   3   4   5   6   7   8   9   10

Respect for authority

1   2   3   4   5   6   7   8   9   10

Taking care of the environment

1   2   3   4   5   6   7   8   9   10

Gratitude

1   2   3   4   5   6   7   8   9   10

Humility

1   2   3   4   5   6   7   8   9   10

Loyalty

1   2   3   4   5   6   7   8   9   10

Compassion (kindness)

1   2   3   4   5   6   7   8   9   10

Worthy accomplishments

1   2   3   4   5   6   7   8   9   10

Honesty in speech and deed

1   2   3   4   5   6   7   8   9   10

Courage

1   2   3   4   5   6   7   8   9   10

Virtue

1   2   3   4   5   6   7   8   9   10

Score_____

Interpreting Your Score

A score less than 124 indicates that the values in this book are not important to you or that you are very weak in your commitment to them. If you scored between **125** and **149** your character in these areas is borderline and if you embrace these values you need character building activities to strengthen your character. If you scored between **150** and **174** your character is o.k., but you should avoid activities that could weaken your character. If you scored between **175** and **199** your character is average with much room for improvement. If you scored between **200** and **224** you have above average character and are a model for others. If you scored between **225** and **239** you are exceptional. If you scored **240** and above you are a virtuous person.

A parting word about character

As you grow older you will find that often values compete

with each other. You might say that our values are always at war with each other. Part of our nature is always pulling in a different direction from the rest of it. Therefore, sometimes we have to assign value to values and choose between them. Some values will be more highly valued than others. At different times in your life, different values will have a higher priority than at other times. The supreme test of character is not just our values and our commitment to them, but the value of the values that we have the greatest commitment to. When Patrick Henry exclaimed, "Give me liberty or give me death," he was choosing between two very important values. He valued life, but he valued freedom more than he valued life without freedom. So if he had to choose between life without freedom, and death, he would choose death.

Fortunately for you, most of your choices will not be that extreme. However, some of them might be pretty serious. You may find out that one of your friends is planning to do something that is dangerous to the school community. You like your friend and want to be loyal to your friendship. But you also have a responsibility to the school community and to the larger society. You will have to decide which value you are going to honor—your loyalty to your friend, or your responsibility to the school and your citizenship. Competing values are really a test of character.

Recently I heard of a young man who put off being drafted into the National Football League to join the Marines and serve in Iraq. He valued fulfilling his duty to the country more highly than he valued the glamor of the N.F.L. Of course, he was hoping that he could do both, but by choosing to do the one first, he was taking a chance that he would never get a chance to do the other. But in taking that chance, he elevated himself in the eyes of those who believe that patriotism is more important than glamor.

Throughout your life you will be balancing some of your values, but some will remain constant. Eventually the things that you hold the greatest value for will win out. That's where character is defined.

Those people who give the greatest amount of their time and life to those values that society deems most important and holds in highest regard are said to have greater character. If we value integrity more than we value winning, the person who chooses to lose rather than win unfairly will be said to have more noble character. In him, the higher value will have won. So, in addition to choosing your values at this point in your life, you have the task of assigning importance to them, or putting a value on the value.

In the end, we all might have some value for the same group of values; what distinguishes people is the priority that those values hold in their value system, and the commitment they have to them. Most students generally value good grades, but for some the value is not high enough to commit to the studying necessary to make good grades. Many students value being star athletes, but some do not value it enough to commit to the long hours of practice necessary to make it happen. The greatest characters are not just those who choose a great set of values, but those who commit to them strongly enough that their lives are defined by them.

A lot of countries value some of the same principles that we Americans value: freedom, justice, and equality, but only in America do we stand ready daily to give our lives to maintain these qualities, and we would die rather than have it any other way. A lot of the people your age will say that they value the twenty-five values covered in this book. At this point you will not be able to tell the depth of their commitment to any of these values. You do not even know the depth of your own commitment. But time will tell, and time will be the ultimate test of your character. One thing is sure, one day you will be what you are in the process of becoming.

Character Building Activities for the Home

1. Helping with the chores.
2. Helping care for younger siblings (without pay).
3. Saying thanks after receiving a gift or kind deed (writing thank you notes when appropriate).
4. Taking responsibility for a pet you wanted.
5. Being quiet in the house while a baby or parent sleeps.
6. Doing homework.
7. Getting permission to play with siblings' toys or wear their clothes.
8. Participating in family functions.
9. Paying back loans.
10. Paying for losses you caused to others' property.
11. Repeating activities or chores until they are done properly.

Character Building Activities for the School

1. Obeying the rules of the school.
2. Keeping the school environment clean.
3. Supporting teachers and staff.
4. Doing school work.
5. Not cheating or getting others to do one's work.
6. Doing volunteer work.
7. Doing activities that protect the environment.
8. Attending all classes and being on time.
9. Not asking for special favors or demanding special treatment.
10. Respecting teachers and classmates.
12. Participating in a sport.
13. Befriending a student who is different or unpopular.

William Jenkins was born in Greenville, Mississippi, where he received his early education. In 1968 he graduated from Jackson State University, Jackson, Mississippi, with a degree in English literature. He taught humanities two years at Uticah Junior College, and started a radio program which was eventually heard in fourteen southern states. Jenkins became a prominent figure in the Civil Rights Movement. Five years after graduating from college, and becoming prominent in civil rights and the ministry, William Jenkins left Mississippi to attend school in Indianapolis. It was a move that was to start the second part of his journey toward making this nation a better place for all of its citizens. After studying at Butler University and Christian Theological Seminary, Jenkins moved to Missouri. In the thirty years since, William Jenkins, through his teaching, lecturing, and personal interaction, has influenced for good the lives of untold numbers of Americans. As a classroom teacher for twenty one years, three years in St. Louis City and eighteen years in the Parkway School District, he impacted the lives and values of thousands of students. Many of them are in regular contact with him to this day and still seek his counsel on issues of importance to them. His books are a rich source of information and inspiration for people from all walks of life. His lectures are moving presentations that appeal to the very best in human nature and the American character.

William Jenkins embodies and advocates the cherished values of the American people. His life has been shaped by preachers and teachers, the two groups most responsible for defining and perpetuating our values. It seems ironic, or poetic justice that William Jenkins, born in a place and at a time when people of his race were deprived of equal access to the American dream, has become one of the most eloquent articulators of that dream and one of the best examples of the values upon which it rests. His life is a testimonial both to the power of our values and the greatness of our country.

William Jenkins Enterprises
P. O. Box 15134
St. Louis, MO 63110
Web Site www.jenkinsedex.com
E-mail: wisdom@mvp.net

Thanks for your purchase and please use this order form to order additional copies of **The Good Book: Character is the Thing**. Single copies are $10.00 plus $2.00 shipping and handling. Ten to fifty copies are $8.00 each. Fifty copies and above are $7.00 a copy. When ordering in bulk estimate shipping at .25 per book.

Vendor's T.T.N.
Purchase Order NO.
Singe copy_____$10.00
Ten to 49 copies_____ $8.00
50 or more copies_____$7.00
Number of Copies_____
Number of books_____
Cost of book_____
Amount enclosed/Due_____

Name_____
Address_____

_____
_____

Telephone_____FAX_____

It is strongly suggested that people who use this book also read **A Little Book For Big People** by William Jenkins. The price and ordering instructions are the same for both books.